Rookie
Read-About®
Community

A Day with Mail Carriers

by Jodie Shepherd

Content Consultant

John McDevitt, Postmaster, Ardsley, New York, Post Office

Reading Consultant

Jeanne Clidas, Ph.D.
Reading Specialist

Children's Press®
An Imprint of Scholastic Inc.
New York Toronto London Auckland Sydney
Mexico City New Delhi Hong Kong
Danbury, Connecticut

Library of Congress Cataloging-in-Publication Data
Shepherd, Jodie.
  A day with mail carriers / by Jodie Shepherd.
      p. cm. — (Rookie read-about community)
  Includes index.
  ISBN 978-0-531-28953-2 (library binding) — ISBN 978-0-531-29253-2 (pbk.)
  1. Letter carriers—Juvenile literature. I. Title.
HE6241.S54 2013
383'.145—dc23   2012013355

Produced by Spooky Cheetah Press

1 2 3 4 5 6 7 8 9 10 R 22 21 20 19 18 17 16 15 14 13

Photographs © 2013: age fotostock/Roy Morsch: 27; Alamy Images/Mark Boulton:
15; Corbis Images/Design Pics: 7, 20 (Don Hammond), 23 (Leah Warkentin); Getty
Images: cover (Flip Chalfant), 28 (Scott Peterson), 16 (Taxi); iStockphoto: 11 (Doug
Schneider), 12 (Naomi Bassitt); Media Bakery: 19 (Cohen/Ostrow), 4, 31 top left
(Glyn Jones); Shutterstock, Inc.: 8 (altafulla), 31 bottom right (Brendan Howard),
24 (Stephen Coburn), 3 top, 31 bottom left (studio online); Thinkstock/iStockphoto:
3 bottom, 31 top right.

Table of Contents

Meet a Mail Carrier 5

From Pencil to Post Office .. 9

Delivering the Mail 18

Many Kinds of Mail 25

Be a Community Helper! 30

Words You Know 31

Index 32

Facts for Now 32

About the Author 32

uniform

mail

mailbag

4

Meet a Mail Carrier

Look around your neighborhood. You might see mail carriers hard at work.

Mail carriers deliver the mail to homes and offices.

From Pencil to Post Office

Want to send a letter to a friend? Put it in an envelope. Then write your friend's name and address on the envelope.

Put a stamp on the envelope. Then drop it into a mailbox. What happens next?

A mail carrier collects all the letters. He takes them to the post office.

At big post offices, most mail is sorted by machine. The sorted mail is sent to smaller post offices for delivery.

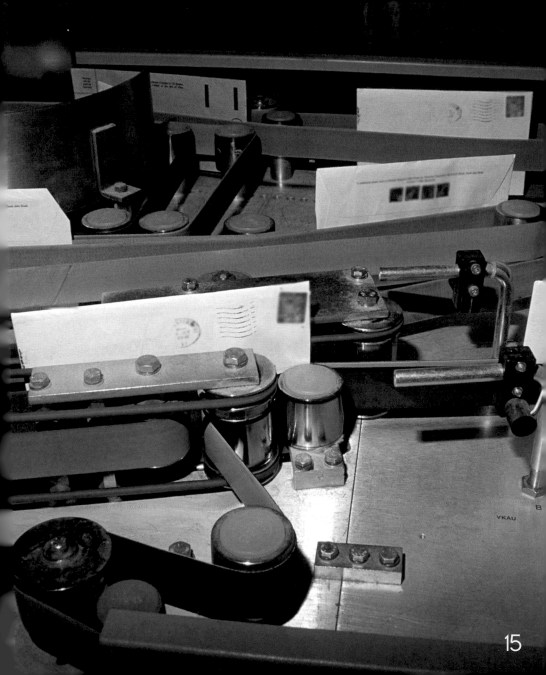

VKAU

15

Packages must be sorted, too.

Delivering the Mail

The mail carrier gets ready for the morning route. He loads the mail into a mailbag. Time to go!

The mail carrier delivers mail to houses on one side of the street and then on the other side.

Then the mail carrier moves to a new street.

23

Many Kinds of Mail

The mail carrier is finished. Now people get to open their mail. It can be a present.

It can be letters, magazines, and cards.

It can be a special delivery that makes someone smile!

Try It! Read page 9 again. Mail a letter to a friend. Do not forget to write your friend's address on the front of the envelope. Put your address at the top left. Attach a stamp and drop your letter into the nearest mailbox.

Be a Community Helper!

- When sending a letter, write the address clearly on the envelope.

- Remember to include the zip code and a return address, too.

- Put the correct stamp on the envelope.

- Never put anything other than mail in a mailbox.

mail carrier

mailbox

package

stamp

Index

address 9, 29

cards 26

envelope 9, 10, 29

letters 9, 13, 26, 29

magazines 26

mailbox 10, 29

packages 17

post office 9, 13, 14

route 18

stamp 10, 29

Facts for Now

Visit this Scholastic Web site for more information on mail carriers:
www.factsfornow.scholastic.com
Enter the keywords **Mail Carriers**

About the Author

Jodie Shepherd, who also writes under the name Leslie Kimmelman, is an award-winning author of dozens of books for children, both fiction and nonfiction. She is also a children's book editor.